1 MONTH OF
FREE
READING

at
www.ForgottenBooks.com

By purchasing this book you are
eligible for one month membership to
ForgottenBooks.com, giving you
unlimited access to our entire
collection of over 1,000,000 titles via
our web site and mobile apps.

To claim your free month visit:
www.forgottenbooks.com/free171458

ISBN 978-0-364-11251-9
PIBN 10171458

COLONEL
EDWARD BUNCOMBE,

FIFTH NORTH CAROLINA

CONTINENTAL REGIMENT.

HIS LIFE, MILITARY CAREER, AND DEATH WHILE A
WOUNDED PRISONER IN PHILADELPHIA DUR-
ING THE WAR OF THE REVOLUTION.

ADDRESS DELIVERED BEFORE THE NORTH CAROLINA SOCIETY OF
THE CINCINNATI AT ITS MEETING HELD IN HILLS-
BOROUGH, JULY 4, 1901.

BY

MARSHALL DeLANCEY HAYWOOD.

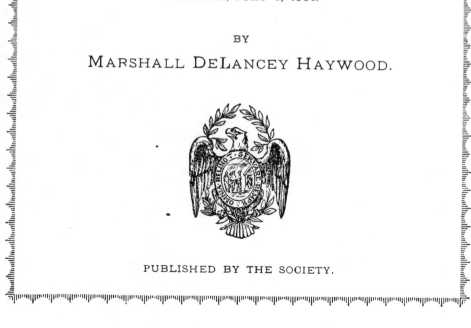

PUBLISHED BY THE SOCIETY.

COLONEL

EDWARD BUNCOMBE,

FIFTH NORTH CAROLINA

CONTINENTAL REGIMENT.

HIS LIFE, MILITARY CAREER, AND DEATH WHILE A
WOUNDED PRISONER IN PHILADELPHIA DUR-
ING THE WAR OF THE REVOLUTION.

ADDRESS DELIVERED BEFORE THE NORTH CAROLINA SOCIETY OF
THE CINCINNATI AT ITS MEETING HELD IN HILLS-
BOROUGH, JULY 4, 1901.

BY

MARSHALL DeLANCEY HAYWOOD.

PUBLISHED BY THE SOCIETY.

RALEIGH:
ALFORD, BYNUM & CHRISTOPHERS, PRINTERS,
1901.

ADDRESS.

Mr. President and Gentlemen of the Society:

It is no small privilege which the North Carolina Society of the Cincinnati enjoys when it meets in this ancient Revolutionary capital, for here our organization was first brought into being. The year of grace 1783, which is the date of its birth, was one of mingled joy and depression to the people of America. The war, it is true, had been fought to a successful close; and, by a treaty wherein they were separately specified, King George had acknowledged the thirteen colonies to be "free, sovereign, and independent States." But how changed was the order of things! The desolation following in the wake of war was scarcely less terrible than war itself, and no State had made greater sacrifices for the cause of liberty than North Carolina. Under daring partisan leaders at home, under Washington in the north, and Greene in the south, her sons had in countless fights lengthened the list of killed and wounded, while those who were spared came home to prove that—

> " Peace hath her victories
> No less renown'd than war."

Yet many, so many, there were of the brave defenders of America who did not return, and their mortal remains still rest on and about the old battlefields made memorable by their valor. To this class belonged the good and gallant officer of whom I shall speak today.

Colonel Edward Buncombe, of Buncombe Hall, in the Colony of North Carolina, was born in the year 1742, on the Island of St. Christopher, sometimes called St. Kitt's, which is one of the Leeward group in the West Indies. The register of St. Ann's Parish, in the above island, shows that: "Edward, son of Thomas and Esther Buncombe," was baptized on the 23d of September in the above year.

Thomas Buncombe, the father of Edward, was a gentleman of English birth and ancestry, and died in the Fall of 1747. He had four children: John, Edward (of whom this sketch treats), Sarah, who married first a Mr. Beach and then a Mr. Humbergen, and Ann, who married a Mr. Caines.

Joseph Buncombe, a brother of Thomas, and hence an uncle of Edward, lived for a time in North Carolina and married Ann, a daughter of George Durant; but he is said to have died while absent from the colony on a visit to relatives. When in North Carolina, his home was in what is now the county of Washington (then a part of Tyrrell), where he owned a valuable estate. He probably died childless, for his property was bequeathed by him to his nephew. The latter, upon viewing the lands in Tyrrell, was so well pleased with them that he disposed of his West Indian possessions and settled permanently in North Carolina about the year 1768. Shortly after this, the mansion known as Buncombe Hall was erected on the site of his uncle's former residence.

Buncombe Hall lay about twelve miles south of Edenton, across Albemarle Sound. At present a small hamlet called Chesson, in Washington County, marks the place where it stood. It was famed throughout the colony as a seat of boundless hospitality. Over an arched gateway, through which the grounds were entered, was inscribed the couplet—

" Welcome all,
To Buncombe Hall."

Not only North Carolinians, but travellers in general, frequently sought shelter there (for it was on a road largely used), and a warm reception awaited each visitor.   In 1773, when Josiah Quincey, of Massachusetts, was returning from a southern tour, he made this entry in his Diary,* while at New Bern, on the 2d of April: " Judge Howard waited upon me in the evening with recommendatory letters to Colonel Palmer of Bath, and Colonel Buncombe of Tyrrell County."   Referring to April 5, he says: " Breakfasted with Colonel Buncombe who waited upon me to Edenton Sound, and gave me letters to his friends there.   Spent this and the next day in crossing Albemarle Sound and in dining and conversing in company with the most celebrated lawyers of Edenton."

Not long after his arrival in North Carolina, Colonel Buncombe was made a magistrate, and served as one of the Justices of the Inferior Court of Tyrrell County. He seems to have been very punctual in the discharge of his official duties ; for, in a letter written on November 29, 1771, by Thomas Jones to Sir Nathaniel Dukinfield, a member of the Governor's Council, the former says says that at a recent court Colonel Buncombe and John McKildoe were the only members present.† Mr. Jones adds: " The people attended with becoming decency and patience but at length grew clamorous, damn'd the absent Justices (I think with propriety), and then prevailed upon McKildoe to adjourn court."

In August, 1892, the centennial of Buncombe County, North Carolina, was celebrated at Asheville, the county-seat.   At that time a sketch of Colonel Buncombe, written by one of his descendants, Mrs. Walter H. Rogers (born Goelet), of New Orleans, appeared in the

---

*Me i oi i of t i e Life of Josia i Qui i cey, Ju i., by i is so i Josia i Qui i cey, pp. 120, 121.

† Colonial Reco i ds of No i t i Ca i oli i a, Vol. IX., p. 60.

Asheville Citizen, and from it we extract the following concerning his residence: "Buncombe Hall, like its founder, has passed away. It remained in the family till after the last war. Ere we quit the subject, let me describe this historic spot. The main building, L shape, contained eight large rooms, and a four-room basement under the whole, which served as store-rooms and a kitchen. The brick used in the building was brought from England. All necessary out-houses, including offices, were upon the premises. The yard was filled on one side with the most beautiful flowers and evergreens; on the other, with fine trees and velvety grass. To the south, stretched away a large peach and apple orchard — the whole surrounded by broad fields under cultivation, set in a back-ground of forests. Here the contemplative mind might revel in historic thought. The old hall, with its lofty ceilings, high oak panels, and chimney casings, seemed to whisper secrets of revolutionary times. Over the door of the dining-room hung the coat-of-arms of the Goelet family (a rising swan on a helmet); and, on the walls, were family portraits of Colonel Buncombe, his sister Mrs. Caines and her little daughter.* On a closet door still remained traces of sealing wax, used by the Colonel in sealing up his silver plate and valuables when he went to the war — vain precaution! His agent, left in charge, turned Tory, robbed him of not only the contents of this closet, but sold off his slaves and valuable timber and then decamped.

"Soon after the fall of Roanoke Island, the Federal soldiers took possession of Plymouth. Then Buncombe Hall fell a prey to them, as Dr. Edward Buncombe Haughton, its owner, was fighting on the Confederate side. He returned after the war, bankrupt

* These portraits were afterwards destroyed in a fire when the residence of Dr. Edward H. Goelet, of Goldsborough, N. C., was burned.—M. DeL. H.

in purse, as all good Southerners were, and the old hall was sold to a Connecticut carpet-bagger. It could even then have been restored to its former greatness, but he razed it to the ground and did not leave a brick standing. It passed, again, out of his possession. The Southern Goelets, all descendants of Colonel Buncombe, were left too poor by the war to rescue his home from annihilation ; and so passed away, and was wantonly destroyed, Buncombe Hall.''

Before proceeding with my narrative, justice requires that acknowledgement be made to Mrs. Rogers, not only for the above quoted passages, but also for the letters hereinafter given, and other items relative to the family connection of her distinguished ancestor.

There are now nine localities in the United States called Buncombe, most (if not all) of which derive the name either directly or indirectly from Colonel Buncombe. They are : Buncombe County, North Carolina ; Buncombe, in Johnson County, Illinois ; Buncombe, in Dubuque County, Iowa — and Buncombe Township, in Sioux County, in the same State ; Buncombe, in Union County, Mississippi ; Buncombe, in Lafayette County, Wisconsin ; Buncombe Ridge, in Lawrence County, Arkansas ; Buncombe, in Knott County, Kentucky; and Buncombe, in Jackson County, Oregon.

The word "buncombe" — which dictionaries give as signifying a bombastic utterance, usually employed in windy harangues to gain popular favor — had its origin through the following circumstance : In the Congress of the United States, between the years 1817 and 1823, the mountain district of North Carolina was represented by the Honorable Felix Walker many of whose constituents were denizens of the now famous county of Buncombe. One day, as Mr. Walker sat pondering over his past political career, he remembered that during that session he had made very few speeches — and this, by the way, was almost as rare a fault with Congressmen in those days as it is now. So he decided to speak; he did speak; he spoke at considerable length ; and he didn't have anything particular to say, but he kept on talking, nevertheless. And when, at last, patience had ceased to be a virtue, and some of his long-suffering colleagues were beginning to leave the hall, he told the more polite members who remained that they might go, too, if they wished, for he intended to have his remarks published and sent to the home people, as the speech was not intended for the House, but *only for Buncombe!*

But to return to Colonel Edward Buncombe. He received his education in Great Britain ; and, while living in St. Christopher, was united in marriage (April 10, 1766,) with Elizabeth Dawson Taylor, who accompanied him to North Carolina, but died just prior to the outbreak of the Revolution. She and her son Thomas are buried under St. Paul's Church, at Edenton. The children of Colonel Buncombe by his marriage with Miss Taylor were:

I. Elizabeth Taylor Buncombe, born on the Island of St. Christopher, March 11, 1767, who was brought when an infant to North Carolina. Her education was received in New York and New Jersey, under the direction of Abraham Lott. She married John Goelet, of New York (afterwards of North Carolina), and left numerous descendants.

II. Thomas Buncombe, born in North Carolina, February 3, 1769, who died young.

III. Hester Ann Buncombe, born April 25, 1771, who married John Clark, of Bertie County, North Carolina, and had two children : Thomas Clark, and

Ann Booth Pollock Clark (wife of John Cox).* Both Thomas Clark and his sister Mrs. Cox died without issue.

From the above it will be seen that the only descendants now living of Colonel Buncombe are through his eldest daughter who married John Goelet, of New York. Mr. Goelet was of Huguenot descent, born in 1759, on the date of the fall of Quebec, and himself saw service in the Revolution. After the war was over and he had married Miss Buncombe, he removed with his wife (about 1791) to Buncombe Hall, and died there in the ninety-fifth year of his age, October, 1853.

In the sketch by Mrs. Rogers, heretofore quoted, she says: "With the death of Colonel Buncombe, the name died in this country, though his patriotic spirit survived, he having eight great-grandsons who volunteered in the Confederate army, one of whom, John Buncombe Goelet, died on Malvern Hill in defence of Richmond, Virginia. He was color-bearer of the Third Alabama Regiment, and belonged to Company A, Mobile Cadets."

Prior to the Revolution, Colonel Buncombe held a commission in the military establishment of the colony. He commanded a regiment of the provincial troops of North Carolina, in the county of Tyrrell.† Like nearly all of the better element of North Carolinians — such men as Robert Howe, Richard Caswell, Francis Nash, Thomas Polk, Alexander Lillington, Griffith Rutherford, and others who afterwards won fame in the Revolution — he used every effort to aid Governor Tryon in suppressing the excesses and riots of the Regulators, and received the official thanks of

* Mrs. Ann Booth Pollock Cox is interred in the old burial ground of St. Paul's Church, Edenton, N. C. On her monument is an elaborate inscription relative to the military record of her grandfather Colonel Buncombe.

†Colonial Records of N. C., Vol. VIII, pp. 705, 707.

His Excellency for the "truly public spirit" displayed by him in the prosecution of this work. He did not, however personally participate in the Alamance campaign, as the regiments of his section of the colony were not called into active service.

In religion, Colonel Buncombe was a member of the Church of England, and, when he left the West Indies, a chaplain is said to have accompanied his household to North Carolina.

In the several years preceding the outbreak of the Revolution, the patriots of North Carolina were boldly prej aring for any emergency which might arise. As early as April 26, 1774, William Hooper had asserted in a letter addressed to Judge Iredell, that the colonies were "striding fast to independence, and ere long would build an empire upon the ruins of Great Britain; would adopt its constitution purged of its impurities, and from an experience of its defects guard against those evils which had wasted its vigor and brought it to an untimely end."* These were troublous times— times calling for men of high purpose and courageous bearing, who, in the face of King, Parliament and Royal Governor, would boldly contend for the rights which were as dear to them as to the people of England. Nor was courage alone sufficient to cope with King George's representatives in Carolina. Political dexterity played no small part in the controversies of that day. Some years prior to the time of which we treat, when the British Parliament passed the Stamp Act, more resistance, and armed resistance, too, was encountered in North Carolina than anywhere else. But no resistance came from the Assembly, for Governor Tryon prorogued that body to prevent official action. This prorogation also prevented the Assembly from later electing delegates to what is known as the

*Defence of North Carolina, by Jo. Seawell Jones, p. 314.

Stamp Act Congress. Tryon's trickery worked so well that his successor, Governor Josiah Martin, decided to play a similar game in 1774. A controversy arising over the laws establishing courts in the colony, and the King's instructions being at variance with the ideas of the Assembly, that body refused to yield; and Governor Martin thereupon put a stop to proceedings by proroguing it. He also determined not to re-convene it until the members were more inclined to obey the royal will. This latter purpose being divulged by the governor's private secretary to John Harvey, that bold statesman determined that an independent assembly, or convention, should be called. He left New Bern, the seat of government, and, on the third of April, discussed the matter with Willie Jones. The night following found him at Buncombe Hall, in the county of Tyrrell. At this place Mr. Harvey confided his plan to Samuel Johnston and Colonel Buncombe.* These notables were impressed with the gravity of the situation, and the night was far spent ere their consultation came to an end. Referring to this conference, in his History of North Carolina,† Moore says: "Buncombe was impulsive and impressionable, but Johnston was the embodiment of caution and deliberation. He was full of determination to resist Lord North's measures, but he feared the effects of too much popular power. These eminent men, with Hooper, John Ashe, Caswell, Person, and others, at once acceded to Harvey's proposition, and the ball of the Revolution was put in motion."

Despite Governor Martin's frantic proclamation forbidding its meeting, the independent convention gathered in New Bern on the 25th of August, 1774.‡

*Defence of North Carolina. by Jo. Seawell Jones, p. 124.

†Vol. I., p. 163.

‡ Colonial Records of N. C., Vol. IX., p. 1041.

No assembly of its kind had ever before convened in America. It was followed by others of like character. Delegates to the Continental Congress were elected. The breach with Great Britain became wider, and finally, as a last resort, independence was declared. And it may be well just here to observe that North Carolina was the very first colony to authorize a national declaration of independence, when in the Provincial or State Congress at Halifax on April 12, 1776, Cornelius Harnett submitted a committee report (which was unanimously adopted), setting forth a resolution : "that the delegates for this colony in the Continental Congress be impowered to concur with the delegates of the other colonies in *declaring indepen-dency.*" This was more than a month before the passage of the famous Virginia resolutions; and even those who question the genuineness of the Mecklenburg Declaration of Independence have never attempted to disprove the authenticity of this resolution adopted by the Provincial Congress at Halifax. So North Carolina will ever claim the proud distinction of having been first to move for independence, as she was also first to offer resistance to the Stamp Act. The preamble to the above resolve in favor of independence is a masterly vindication of the course pursued by the colonies, and should be read of all men.*

As well may be supposed, a man of Colonel Buncombe's spirit and patriotism was not the person to hold back from participation in a war, however perilous, which he himself had been instrumental in bringing about. On September 9, 1775, he was elected Colonel of the militia forces of Tyrrell County† by the Provincial Congress of North Carolina, then in session at

---

* For full text of preamble and resolutions, see Colonial Records of N. C., Vol. X., p. 512; Defence of North Carolina, by Jo. Seawell Jones, p. 251.

† Colonial Records of N. C., Vol. X,, p. 205.

Halifax. He fulfilled the duties of this position for about seven months, and, on the 17th of April, 1776, was transferred to the regular service, being made Colonel of the Fifth Regiment of North Carolina troops in the Continental Line.* During the period intervening between its organization and the time when ordered to the field, the Fifth Regiment was maintained at his private expense. On May 7, 1776, the appointment of Colonel Buncombe was confirmed by the Continental Congress,† and his regiment was assigned to General Francis Nash's brigade This brigade was made up at Wilmington, North Carolina, in the Summer of 1776, and remained in that vicinity till November of the same year. Having been ordered to join Washington's army, then operating in the north, General Nash and his troops set out from Wilmingtou about the 15th of November, and, on reaching the town of Halifax, were ordered back south, the object being to keep the British from entering Georgia by way of St. Augustine. No sooner, however, had Charleston been reached, than orders were again countermanded. Thereupon the brigade marched to Haddrell's Point, opposite Fort Sullivan, South Carolina, at which place it remained in the forces which were there opposing the operations of Sir Henry Clinton. In March, 1777, orders were again given the North Carolina brigade to join Washington. Moving up through North Carolina and Virginia, and crossing the Potomac near Alexandria, the main army was finally reached on the Jersey side of the Delaware River, at Middlebrook. The accession of these brave North Carolinians was gladly hailed by Washington, and they were given a thundering welcome in the shape of

---

* Colonial Records of N. C., Vol. X., p. 520.

† American Archives (4th Series), Vol. V., p. 1698.

"a salutation of thirteen cannon, each fired thirteen times."*

At Alexandria, in the latter part of May, the march of Nash's brigade had been delayed to inoculate the troops against small-pox.

Early in July, the North Carolinians, together with the other troops around Philadelphia, were detailed to complete the fortifications on the Delaware River.†

On the 14th of August, 1777, while the Continental forces were in camp at Trenton, we find Colonel Buncombe and the other field-officers of Nash's brigade uniting in a protest against a Pennsylvanian, Colonel Edward Hand, being made a brigadier-general to command North Carolina troops, *vice* General James Moore, who had recently died.‡ While not questioning Colonel Hand's merit, they declared that the appointment of any outsider would be a "reflection on North Carolina and a stab at military honour throughout the continent in general." The memorial also contained some rather unpleasant references to Thomas Burke (then a delegate from North Carolina in the Continental Congress), and charged him with neglecting the interests of the State he represented to advance one of his own countrymen — he and Hand both being natives of Ireland. Burke was so enraged thereby that he declared, referring to the signers of the protest: "Their behaviour in this instance has determined me to forego all particular attention to them. I hope they will so distinguish themselves that their merit alone will be sufficient for their promotion, without standing in need of any assistance which I could give." Whether Doctor Burke did forego all particular at-

---

* This account of the movements of Nash's brigade is partly from narrative of Hugh McDonald in old series of North Carolina University Magazine (1853-'56, II., 466-470; IV.. 158-162; V.. 28-31. 208-211, 360-363), and partly from State Records.

† State Records of N. C.. Vol. XI., p. 733.

‡ State Records of N. C., Vol. XI., pp. 562, 750.

tention to the North Carolinians does not appear, but he certainly succeeded in his efforts to secure the promotion of Hand, who, it is a pleasure to add, rendered long and honorable service during the war, and held a major-general's commission in the regular army after the return of peace.

On the 11th day of September, 1777, was fought the battle of Brandywine, and here Colonel Buncombe's regiment was actively engaged. In this conflict, the North Carolina brigade and Greene's division were ranged in the centre of the American Army.* Being ordered to support the right wing (then sorely pressed), their absence left the troops under General Wayne to cope alone with a vastly superior force of the enemy. After a brave and bloody resistance, Wayne was forced to retire, and the day was lost.

After his reverses at Brandywine, the never-despairing Washington drew together his forces and prepared again to attack. He was, in truth, a leader whom no disaster could appall.

The next scene of action was at Germantown, Pennsylvania. This fight occurred on the 4th of October, and was destined to be Colonel Buncombe's last battle, for there he received the wound which ultimately caused his death while a prisoner in the hands of the British. The brigade of North Carolinians was selected by the commander-in-chief to act as a part of the reserve corps at Germantown, but it may be questioned if it would have suffered more terribly if placed in the van. The brave General Nash, with his thigh shattered by a solid shot,† and fainting from the loss of blood, was borne to a near-by house and lingered only

---

* State Records of N. C., Vol. XI. page 621.

† Moore's History (I., 243, NOTE) states upon the authority of my father, the late Dr. Richard B. Haywood, that Col. William Polk said that Gen. Nash received his mortal wound from a shot through the eyes. That Col. Polk also made this statement to persons other than Dr. Haywood appears in Dr. W. M. Polk's biography of Bishop Polk (I. 27), which quotes Col. Polk as as saying Nash "was blind," and almost in syncope from loss of blood. Yet, strange as it may seem, though official

three days.   Lieutenant-Colonel Henry Irwin of Buncombe's regiment (the Fifth), Captain Jacob Turner
of the Third, and Lieutenant John McCann of the
Sixth North Carolina, lay dead on the field.   Major
William Polk of the Ninth, received a shot in the
face, which, for a time, deprived him of the power
of speech.   Captain John Armstrong of the Second,
Lieutenant Joshua Hadley of the Sixth, and Ensign
John Daves of the Second, were also among the
wounded, as were doubtless many others, of whom,
unfortunately, we have now no record.

And the privates!   How many of those forgotten
heroes shed their blood and gave up their lives, as
freely as did the officers, will never be known.   May
their devotion be rewarded in a better world.

> " 'Tis to the virtue of such men, man owes
>   His portion in the good that heaven bestows;
> And when recording history displays
>   Feats of renown, though wrought in ancient days—
> Tells of a few stout hearts that fought, and died,
>   Where duty placed them, at their country's side—
> The man that is not moved with what he reads,
>   That takes not fire at their heroic deeds,
> Unworthy of the blessings of the brave,
>   Is base in kind, and born to be a slave."

When struck down on the field of Germantown,
Colonel Buncombe was left for dead by the retreating

records show he was himself present and severely wounded at Germantown, Col. Polk was mistaken in this, as will now be shown. John Penn, writing from near the battlefield (on Oct. 10th) only three days after Nash's death, says: " Poor General Nash was killed by a cannon ball, with his horse." An obituary published in the NORTH CAROLINA GAZETTE, less than a month later (Oct. 31st), states: "The winged Messenger of Death, a cannon ball, * * * * struck him on the thigh, tore his body in a most dreadful manner, and killed his horse under him." In the legisla-tive proceedings in honor of Gen. Nash (Nov. 19th), less than six weeks after his death, it appears that he "received a wound from a cannon ball; and, after lan-guishing some days. * * * * closed his useful life." See State Records of North Carolina, Vol. XI., pp. 649, 789; Ibid., Vol. XII., p. 279. Pennsylvania accounts also say Nash was killed by a cannon ball which struck him on the thigh. The statement by Col. Polk was made when he was a very old man, fifty years or more after the battle; hence his mistake may have been caused by confusing Gen. Nash with some other wounded officer at Germantown who may have been shot through the eyes.   Col. Polk's second wife was a sister of Dr. Haywood's mother.

Americans and lay where he fell until the next day, when a British officer recognized him as an old schoolmate and had him removed to Philadelphia. There he was paroled within the city limits. His wound at first yielded to treatment, and it was thought he would recover. But as life dragged on, he realized that the weakened state of his constitution could not longer withstand continued privation. Being in great financial straits, and his physical condition growing worse day by day, he at last applied to Sir William Howe, the British commandant of Philadelphia, for leave to go as a paroled prisoner either to England or to North Carolina; but, if this request was ever granted, he did not avail himself of the privilege. Fearing that the motives which prompted his application had been misconstrued, he addressed to General Washington a letter, the original of which is now in possession of the Goelet family, Washington having returned it to one of that connection, after the Revolution, as a memorial of its brave author. Following is the communication in full:

Sir,

As I deem myself accountable to you, as my General, for every part of my conduct, permit this letter to speak what in person I cannot deliver.

Distressed I have been, repeatedly soliciting a supply of money from camp, yet hitherto I have not been obliged. I never was accustomed to adversity. Let the feelings of Your Excellency's heart speak for me.

It is true I have my failings. Human nature will operate no perfection. But, as an officer, have I in any shape or respect disgraced my regiment? Have I not been anxious to fight for America? Can one of Your Excellency's officers accuse me of cowardice?

Prompted by my distress, I was inevitably compelled to apply to His Excellency General Sir William Howe either for a parole to the southward or to Britain. Here I cannot command hard money; there I can.

The exigency of my case, I am persuaded, will point out the expediency of my adopted measure. I request that you will not think my departure from America a desertion of it. Always amenable to my General's call, in six months I shall be ready to obey your orders if you think proper to have me exchanged.

I have the honor to be, with sincerity, Your Excellency's
Very respectful and obed't serv't,

E. BUNCOMBE.

To
His Excellency
General Washington,
Commander-in-Chief
of the Forces of the United Colonies.

The unfortunate captive, by whom this letter was written, never lived to enjoy the freedom he so much loved. He was, at times, addicted to somnambulism; and about the middle of May, 1778, while walking in his sleep, fell down a flight of stairs. This accident caused his wound to open afresh; and, before assistance could avail, he bled to death.

Thus passed the spirit of Edward Buncombe, soldier and gentleman—

> " Than whom, knight
> Was never dubbed, more bold in fight;
> Nor, when from war and armor free,
> More famed for stately courtesy."

And when they buried him, an entry was made on the parish-register of Christ Church, Philadelphia, noting the interment of *Cornelius* Buncombe; while many North Carolina historians, in later years, have given his first name as Richard! This consideration for his memory brings to mind Byron's remark on reading of the death, at Waterloo, of an old college-mate: "There is fame! A man is killed. His name is Grose, and they print it Grove."

The death of Colonel Buncombe occurred at the house of a Mrs. Kendall. This we learn from a letter written on July 22, 1778, by Thomas Franklin, a Philadelphia Quaker, to General Benedict Arnold (then in the American service), giving a list of Buncombe's effects, ''left in ye hands of ye widow Edy Kendall, where he lodged last and died.''

During Colonel Buncombe's service in the army, he was accompanied by a faithful slave, Charles, and to this negro he bequeathed freedom. The following reference to him is found in a letter from the Reverend Adam Boyd, Brigade-Chaplain in the North Carolina Line, dated in camp, at White Plains, New York, August 24, 1778: ''Charles, I believe is entitled to his freedom. The Colonel has often been heard to say he should not serve anyone after his death; and some of his officers have heard him say he had, in his will, ordered him his freedom. A law of our State forbids such emancipation without the consent of the court of that county in which the master usually resides. But an appeal to that law in this case I do not think would be right, because it would defeat the testator's intention, which I think should be held sacred. Though I think it would be easy for his heirs, should they avail themselves of the law, to enslave Charles for life, I hope such a thing will not be attempted. The principal object of this law was to prevent the discharge of slaves that were not able to earn their living — a cruel practice which had scandalously prevailed to avoid paying taxes, from which old age or other infirmities do not exempt slaves.'' The will, by which Charles was supposed to be emancipated, could not be found among Colonel Buncombe's papers, but the negro was allowed to go free in deference to his late owner's expressed wish. The only will found was one which had been made before the war.

The spot where Colonel Buncombe lies buried is not marked, but it is somewhere within the ''additional church-yard'' of the parish of Christ Church, on the corner of Arch and Fifth Streets, Philadelphia. In this enclosure are also deposited the remains of Benjamin Franklin, and other patriots; while not many miles off sleep Nash, Irwin, Turner, McCann, and their brave comrades, who counted not life above liberty. And North Carolina should little grieve that her sons are left on the soil of Pennsylvania. There they fell, fighting for the common cause of America; there let them rest.

> "The neighing troop, the flashing blade,
>   The bugle's stirring blast,
> The charge, the dreadful cannonade,
>   The din and shout are past;
> Nor war's wild note nor glory's peal
>   Shall thrill with fierce delight
> Those breasts that nevermore may feel
>   The rapture of the fight."

As a grateful tribute to the memory of Colonel Buncombe, the General Assembly of North Carolina, at its session of 1791, created a new county just westward of the Blue Ridge Mountains, and called it in his honor. This is a monument which will stand when the proudest memorials of our day have become misshapen masses of stone. For ages it will tell of the brave soldier who fought for his country's freedom and now sleeps in a forgotten grave, awaiting the last summons when the earth and the sea shall give up their dead. Peaceful be his rest! — and may generations yet to come draw inspiration from the life he led.

9 780364 112519